Table of Contents

Introduction 1
Chapter 1: Jollof Rice 2
Chapter 2: Egusi Soup 5
Chapter 3: Bobotie 7
Chapter 4: Chicken Muamba 9
Chapter 5: Bunny Chow 11
Chapter 6: Piri Piri Chicken 13
Chapter 7: Tagine 15
Chapter 8: Injera with Doro Wat 17
Chapter 9: Biltong 20
Chapter 10: Mandazi 22
Chapter 11: Kachumbari 24
Chapter 12: Chakalaka 25
Chapter 13: Moambe Chicken 27
Chapter 14: Groundnut Stew 29
Chapter 15: Braaibroodjies 31
Chapter 16: Fufu and Light Soup 33
Chapter 17: Sosaties 35
Chapter 18: Sambaza 37
Chapter 19: Waakye 39
Chapter 20: Couscous 41
Conclusion 42

Introduction

Welcome to "20 Classic African Dishes," a culinary exploration of Africa's rich and diverse food traditions. Africa is a continent known for its vibrant cultures, each with its own unique culinary identity. This cookbook is a celebration of the traditional dishes that have been passed down through generations, bringing together the tastes, aromas, and colors that define African cuisine.

From the coastal flavors of Morocco's Tagine to the hearty, comforting soups of Nigeria, this collection showcases the variety and depth of African cooking. Whether you are new to African cuisine or looking to expand your culinary repertoire, these recipes are designed to be accessible and enjoyable for cooks of all levels. Each dish is accompanied by step-by-step instructions and helpful tips to ensure your cooking experience is both fun and successful.

As you embark on this culinary journey, you'll discover the stories behind the dishes, the cultural significance of the ingredients, and the techniques that make African cooking so special. Let's dive into the heart of Africa, one delicious dish at a time.

Chapter 1: Jollof Rice

- A flavorful West African dish made with rice, tomatoes, onions, and a blend of spices, often accompanied by vegetables and meats.

Ingredients:

- 3 cups long-grain parboiled rice
- 1/4 cup vegetable oil
- 1 large onion, chopped
- 3 cloves garlic, minced
- 1-inch piece of ginger, grated
- 1 red bell pepper, chopped
- 1 green bell pepper, chopped
- 4 large tomatoes, blended
- 1/4 cup tomato paste
- 2 cups chicken or vegetable broth
- 1 teaspoon thyme
- 1 teaspoon curry powder
- 1 teaspoon smoked paprika
- 1 bay leaf
- Salt and pepper to taste
- 2-3 scotch bonnet peppers (optional, for heat)
- 2 cups mixed vegetables (peas, carrots, green beans)
- 2 cups cooked chicken or any protein of your choice (optional)
- Fresh parsley or cilantro for garnish

Cooking Instructions:

1. **Prepare the Rice**: Rinse the rice in cold water until the water runs clear. Drain and set aside.
2. **Cook the Base**: In a large pot, heat the vegetable oil over medium heat. Add the chopped onions and sauté until translucent.
3. **Add Aromatics**: Add the minced garlic and grated ginger, and cook for another 2 minutes until fragrant.
4. **Incorporate Vegetables**: Add the chopped red and green bell peppers, and cook until they start to soften, about 3-4 minutes.
5. **Tomato Mixture**: Stir in the blended tomatoes and tomato paste. Cook this mixture, stirring occasionally, until it reduces and the oil starts to separate from the tomato mixture (about 10-15 minutes).
6. **Season**: Add the thyme, curry powder, smoked paprika, bay leaf, salt, and pepper. Stir well to combine.
7. **Simmer**: Pour in the chicken or vegetable broth and add the scotch bonnet peppers if using. Bring to a boil.
8. **Cook the Rice**: Add the rinsed rice to the pot, stirring to ensure it is evenly coated with the sauce. Reduce the heat to low, cover the pot with a tight-fitting lid, and simmer for 20-25 minutes.
9. **Add Vegetables and Protein**: Stir in the mixed vegetables and cooked chicken (if using) about 10 minutes before the end of the cooking time. Continue to cook until the rice is tender and the liquid is absorbed.

10. **Fluff and Serve**: Remove the bay leaf and scotch bonnet peppers. Fluff the rice with a fork and garnish with fresh parsley or cilantro. Serve hot.

Chapter 2: Egusi Soup

- A rich Nigerian soup made from melon seeds, leafy vegetables, and various meats or fish, often served with pounded yam or fufu.

Ingredients:

- 2 cups ground egusi (melon seeds)
- 1/4 cup palm oil
- 1 large onion, chopped
- 3 cloves garlic, minced
- 1-inch piece of ginger, grated
- 1 red bell pepper, chopped
- 2 large tomatoes, blended
- 1/2 cup tomato paste
- 6 cups spinach or bitter leaf, chopped
- 1 lb assorted meats (beef, goat, tripe, etc.)
- 1 cup dried fish or stockfish, soaked and deboned
- 2 tablespoons ground crayfish
- 2 scotch bonnet peppers, chopped (optional)
- 1 teaspoon ground ogiri or iru (fermented locust beans)
- Salt and pepper to taste
- 4 cups water or broth

Cooking Instructions:

1. **Prepare the Meats**: In a large pot, boil the assorted meats with salt, pepper, and a chopped onion until tender. Remove the meats from the pot and set aside. Reserve the cooking liquid as stock.

2. **Cook the Base**: In another large pot, heat the palm oil over medium heat. Add the chopped onions and sauté until translucent.
3. **Add Aromatics**: Add the minced garlic and grated ginger, and cook for another 2 minutes until fragrant.
4. **Incorporate Vegetables**: Add the chopped red bell pepper and cook until it starts to soften, about 3-4 minutes.
5. **Tomato Mixture**: Stir in the blended tomatoes and tomato paste. Cook this mixture, stirring occasionally, until it reduces and the oil starts to separate from the tomato mixture (about 10-15 minutes).
6. **Prepare Egusi**: In a bowl, mix the ground egusi with a small amount of water to form a thick paste.
7. **Add Egusi**: Spoon the egusi paste into the pot in small lumps. Allow it to cook undisturbed for a few minutes before stirring.
8. **Combine Ingredients**: Add the reserved meat stock, ground crayfish, scotch bonnet peppers (if using), and ground ogiri or iru. Stir well to combine.
9. **Simmer**: Return the assorted meats and dried fish to the pot. Add more water or broth if needed to achieve the desired consistency. Simmer for 20-30 minutes.
10. **Add Greens**: Stir in the chopped spinach or bitter leaf. Cook for an additional 5-10 minutes until the greens are tender.
11. **Season and Serve**: Adjust seasoning with salt and pepper to taste. Serve hot with fufu, pounded yam, or rice.

Chapter 3: Bobotie

- A South African dish consisting of spiced minced meat baked with an egg-based topping, typically served with yellow rice and chutney.

Ingredients:

- 2 tablespoons vegetable oil
- 2 large onions, finely chopped
- 2 cloves garlic, minced
- 1 1/2 pounds ground beef or lamb
- 2 slices of white bread
- 1/2 cup milk
- 2 tablespoons curry powder
- 1 teaspoon turmeric
- 1 teaspoon ground cumin
- 1 teaspoon ground coriander
- 1/2 teaspoon ground ginger
- 1/2 teaspoon ground cinnamon
- 1/2 cup chutney
- 2 tablespoons lemon juice
- 1 tablespoon sugar
- 1/2 cup raisins
- 1/4 cup slivered almonds (optional)
- Salt and pepper to taste
- 2 large eggs
- 6 bay leaves

Cooking Instructions:

1. **Preheat Oven**: Preheat your oven to 350°F (175°C).
2. **Prepare the Meat Mixture**: Heat the vegetable oil in a large skillet over medium

heat. Add the chopped onions and sauté until golden brown. Add the minced garlic and cook for another 1-2 minutes.
3. **Cook the Meat**: Add the ground beef or lamb to the skillet, breaking it up with a spoon. Cook until browned and no longer pink. Drain any excess fat.
4. **Soak the Bread**: While the meat is cooking, soak the slices of bread in the milk. Once soaked, squeeze out the excess milk and crumble the bread into the meat mixture. Reserve the milk for later.
5. **Add Spices and Ingredients**: Stir in the curry powder, turmeric, cumin, coriander, ground ginger, cinnamon, chutney, lemon juice, sugar, raisins, and almonds. Season with salt and pepper. Mix well to combine all the ingredients.
6. **Prepare for Baking**: Transfer the meat mixture to a greased baking dish, spreading it out evenly.
7. **Egg Mixture**: In a small bowl, beat the eggs with the reserved milk. Pour the egg mixture over the meat in the baking dish. Place the bay leaves on top.
8. **Bake**: Bake in the preheated oven for 30-40 minutes, until the top is golden brown and set.
9. **Serve**: Remove from the oven, discard the bay leaves, and let it cool slightly before serving. Serve with yellow rice or a side of your choice.

Chapter 4: Chicken Muamba

- A popular dish from Angola made with chicken, palm oil, garlic, okra, and chili, creating a hearty and spicy stew.

Ingredients:

- 1 whole chicken, cut into pieces
- 1/4 cup vegetable oil or palm oil
- 2 large onions, finely chopped
- 4 cloves garlic, minced
- 1-inch piece of ginger, grated
- 1 red bell pepper, chopped
- 2 tomatoes, chopped
- 1/2 cup tomato paste
- 1 cup chicken broth or water
- 1/2 cup peanut butter or ground peanuts
- 1/4 cup palm nut cream or sauce (moambe sauce)
- 1-2 scotch bonnet peppers, whole (optional)
- 1 teaspoon smoked paprika
- Salt and pepper to taste
- 1/2 cup chopped spinach or other leafy greens
- Fresh parsley or cilantro for garnish

Cooking Instructions:

1. **Prepare the Chicken**: Season the chicken pieces with salt and pepper. In a large pot, heat the vegetable oil or palm oil over medium-high heat. Brown the chicken pieces on all sides, working in batches if

necessary. Remove the chicken and set aside.
2. **Cook the Aromatics**: In the same pot, add the chopped onions and sauté until golden brown. Add the minced garlic and grated ginger, and cook for another 2-3 minutes until fragrant.
3. **Add Vegetables**: Add the chopped red bell pepper and cook until it starts to soften, about 3-4 minutes.
4. **Tomato Mixture**: Stir in the chopped tomatoes and tomato paste. Cook this mixture, stirring occasionally, until it reduces and the oil starts to separate from the tomato mixture (about 10-15 minutes).
5. **Combine Ingredients**: Return the browned chicken pieces to the pot. Pour in the chicken broth or water and bring to a boil.
6. **Add Peanut Butter**: Reduce the heat to low and stir in the peanut butter or ground peanuts until well combined. Add the palm nut cream or sauce and whole scotch bonnet peppers if using. Add the smoked paprika. Simmer the mixture for about 30 minutes, until the chicken is cooked through and tender.
7. **Finish the Dish**: Stir in the chopped spinach or other leafy greens and cook for an additional 5-10 minutes until the greens are wilted and tender.
8. **Season and Serve**: Adjust seasoning with salt and pepper to taste. Remove the scotch bonnet peppers before serving if a milder dish is desired. Garnish with fresh parsley or cilantro. Serve hot with rice, fufu, or boiled plantains.

Chapter 5: Bunny Chow

- A South African street food favorite, this hollowed-out bread loaf is filled with a spicy curry, often made with lamb, chicken, or vegetables.

Ingredients:

- 1 pound (450g) beef or lamb, cubed
- 2 tablespoons vegetable oil
- 2 large onions, chopped
- 2 cloves garlic, minced
- 1-inch piece of ginger, grated
- 2 tablespoons curry powder
- 1 teaspoon ground cumin
- 1 teaspoon ground coriander
- 1/2 teaspoon turmeric
- 1/2 teaspoon chili powder
- 2 large tomatoes, chopped
- 1/2 cup tomato paste
- 2 cups beef or vegetable broth
- 2 large potatoes, peeled and cubed
- 1 can (15 ounces) chickpeas, drained and rinsed
- Salt and pepper to taste
- 1 loaf of white bread (unsliced)
- Fresh cilantro for garnish

Cooking Instructions:

1. **Prepare the Meat**: In a large pot, heat the vegetable oil over medium-high heat. Add the cubed meat and brown on all sides. Remove the meat and set aside.

2. **Cook the Aromatics**: In the same pot, add the chopped onions and sauté until golden brown. Add the minced garlic and grated ginger, and cook for another 2-3 minutes until fragrant.
3. **Add Spices**: Stir in the curry powder, ground cumin, ground coriander, turmeric, and chili powder. Cook for 1-2 minutes to release the flavors.
4. **Tomato Mixture**: Add the chopped tomatoes and tomato paste. Cook this mixture, stirring occasionally, until it reduces and the oil starts to separate from the tomato mixture (about 10 minutes).
5. **Simmer**: Return the browned meat to the pot. Pour in the beef or vegetable broth and bring to a boil. Reduce the heat to low, cover, and simmer for 45 minutes to 1 hour, or until the meat is tender.
6. **Add Potatoes and Chickpeas**: Add the cubed potatoes and chickpeas to the pot. Continue to simmer until the potatoes are cooked through and tender, about 20-30 minutes.
7. **Prepare the Bread**: Cut the loaf of bread into quarters. Hollow out each quarter, creating a bread bowl, while keeping the removed bread aside.
8. **Serve**: Fill each bread bowl with the curry mixture. Garnish with fresh cilantro and serve with the removed bread pieces for dipping.

Chapter 6: Piri Piri Chicken

- A Mozambican-Portuguese fusion dish, featuring grilled chicken marinated in a spicy piri piri sauce made from chili peppers, garlic, and lemon.

Ingredients:

- 1 whole chicken, spatchcocked (backbone removed and flattened)
- 4 tablespoons olive oil
- 4 cloves garlic, minced
- 1-2 bird's eye chilies, finely chopped (adjust to heat preference)
- 2 tablespoons smoked paprika
- 1 teaspoon cayenne pepper
- 1 teaspoon ground cumin
- 1 teaspoon ground coriander
- 1 teaspoon dried oregano
- Juice of 2 lemons
- 1/4 cup white vinegar
- Salt and pepper to taste
- Fresh cilantro for garnish

Cooking Instructions:

1. **Prepare the Marinade**: In a bowl, combine the olive oil, minced garlic, chopped bird's eye chilies, smoked paprika, cayenne pepper, ground cumin, ground coriander, dried oregano, lemon juice, white vinegar, salt, and pepper. Mix well to create a marinade.
2. **Marinate the Chicken**: Place the spatchcocked chicken in a large resealable

plastic bag or a shallow dish. Pour the marinade over the chicken, ensuring it is well coated. Seal the bag or cover the dish and refrigerate for at least 2 hours, preferably overnight.
3. **Preheat the Grill**: Preheat your grill to medium-high heat.
4. **Grill the Chicken**: Remove the chicken from the marinade and shake off any excess. Place the chicken on the grill, skin side down. Grill for 10-15 minutes per side, or until the internal temperature reaches 165°F (75°C) and the skin is crispy and golden.
5. **Rest the Chicken**: Remove the chicken from the grill and let it rest for 5-10 minutes before carving.
6. **Serve**: Cut the chicken into pieces and garnish with fresh cilantro. Serve with a side of your choice, such as grilled vegetables, rice, or salad.

Chapter 7: Tagine

- A North African dish from Morocco, consisting of slow-cooked meat or vegetables with dried fruits, nuts, and aromatic spices, prepared in a clay pot.

Ingredients:

- 1 lb (450g) lamb or chicken, cut into chunks
- 2 tablespoons olive oil
- 1 large onion, chopped
- 3 cloves garlic, minced
- 1 teaspoon ground ginger
- 1 teaspoon ground cumin
- 1 teaspoon ground cinnamon
- 1 teaspoon ground turmeric
- 1 teaspoon paprika
- 1/2 teaspoon ground black pepper
- 1/4 teaspoon saffron threads (optional)
- 1/4 cup chopped fresh cilantro
- 1/4 cup chopped fresh parsley
- 2 cups chicken or vegetable broth
- 1 cup canned chickpeas, drained and rinsed
- 1 cup dried apricots, chopped
- 1/2 cup pitted green olives
- 1 preserved lemon, chopped (or zest of 1 lemon if unavailable)
- Salt to taste

Cooking Instructions:

1. **Prepare the Meat**: Heat the olive oil in a large tagine or heavy-bottomed pot over medium heat. Add the chopped onions and sauté until golden brown. Add the minced

garlic and cook for another 2-3 minutes until fragrant.
2. **Brown the Meat**: Add the lamb or chicken chunks to the pot, browning them on all sides.
3. **Add Spices**: Stir in the ground ginger, cumin, cinnamon, turmeric, paprika, black pepper, and saffron threads (if using). Mix well to coat the meat evenly with the spices.
4. **Add Broth and Herbs**: Pour in the chicken or vegetable broth and add the chopped cilantro and parsley. Stir to combine.
5. **Simmer**: Bring the mixture to a boil, then reduce the heat to low. Cover and simmer for 1 to 1.5 hours, or until the meat is tender.
6. **Add Remaining Ingredients**: Stir in the chickpeas, chopped dried apricots, green olives, and preserved lemon (or lemon zest). Continue to simmer for an additional 15-20 minutes, allowing the flavors to meld together.
7. **Season and Serve**: Adjust seasoning with salt to taste. Serve the tagine hot with couscous or bread.

Chapter 8: Injera with Doro Wat

- An Ethiopian staple, injera is a spongy flatbread served with doro wat, a spicy chicken stew made with berbere spice and hard-boiled eggs.

Injera Ingredients:

- 2 cups teff flour (or a mix of teff and all-purpose flour)
- 3 cups water
- 1/4 teaspoon salt
- 1/2 teaspoon active dry yeast (optional, for faster fermentation)

Injera Cooking Instructions:

1. **Prepare the Batter**: In a large bowl, combine the teff flour, water, and yeast (if using). Mix well until smooth. Cover the bowl with a clean cloth and let it ferment at room temperature for 1-3 days, until bubbles form and the batter has a slightly sour smell.
2. **Add Salt**: Stir in the salt just before cooking.
3. **Cook the Injera**: Heat a non-stick skillet or a large flat griddle over medium-high heat. Pour a ladleful of batter onto the skillet, spreading it in a thin, even layer. Cook until bubbles form on the surface and the edges begin to lift, about 2-3 minutes. Do not flip. Remove the injera and let it cool on a plate. Repeat with the remaining batter.

Doro Wat Ingredients:

- 1 whole chicken, cut into pieces
- 1/4 cup lemon juice
- 2 large onions, finely chopped
- 1/4 cup vegetable oil or niter kibbeh (Ethiopian spiced butter)
- 4 cloves garlic, minced
- 1-inch piece of ginger, grated
- 2 tablespoons berbere spice mix
- 2 tablespoons paprika
- 1 teaspoon ground cardamom
- 1/2 teaspoon ground fenugreek
- 4 hard-boiled eggs, peeled
- 2 cups chicken broth or water
- Salt to taste

Doro Wat Cooking Instructions:

1. **Marinate the Chicken**: In a large bowl, marinate the chicken pieces with lemon juice and salt. Let it sit for about 30 minutes.
2. **Cook the Onions**: In a large pot, heat the vegetable oil or niter kibbeh over medium heat. Add the finely chopped onions and sauté until they are deeply caramelized, about 20-30 minutes.
3. **Add Aromatics and Spices**: Stir in the minced garlic and grated ginger, cooking for another 2-3 minutes. Add the berbere spice mix, paprika, ground cardamom, and ground fenugreek. Cook for 2-3 minutes until the spices are fragrant.
4. **Add Chicken and Broth**: Add the marinated chicken pieces to the pot, stirring to coat them with the spice mixture. Pour in

the chicken broth or water, bringing the mixture to a simmer. Cover and cook for 45-60 minutes, until the chicken is tender and cooked through.
5. **Add Eggs**: Add the hard-boiled eggs to the pot, allowing them to warm through in the sauce.
6. **Adjust Seasoning**: Adjust the seasoning with salt to taste. Simmer for an additional 10 minutes to let the flavors meld together.
7. **Serve**: Serve the Doro Wat hot, accompanied by injera. Place the injera on a large plate and ladle the Doro Wat over it, allowing the injera to soak up the flavorful sauce.

Chapter 9: Biltong

- A South African dried, cured meat snack similar to jerky, made from beef or game meat and flavored with vinegar, salt, and spices.

Ingredients:

- 2 lbs (900g) beef (silverside or topside cuts are ideal)
- 1/2 cup coarse sea salt
- 2 tablespoons brown sugar
- 1 tablespoon bicarbonate of soda (baking soda)
- 1 tablespoon ground coriander
- 1 tablespoon cracked black pepper
- 1 teaspoon ground cloves
- 1/4 cup apple cider vinegar
- 1/4 cup Worcestershire sauce

Cooking Instructions:

1. **Prepare the Meat**: Trim the beef of any excess fat and sinew. Cut the meat into strips about 1 inch wide and 6-8 inches long.
2. **Season the Meat**: In a bowl, combine the coarse sea salt, brown sugar, bicarbonate of soda, ground coriander, cracked black pepper, and ground cloves. Rub this mixture all over the beef strips, ensuring they are well coated. Let the meat sit for about 30 minutes.
3. **Marinate the Meat**: In a separate bowl, mix the apple cider vinegar and Worcestershire

sauce. Dip each strip of beef into this mixture, then lay them out in a single layer in a dish. Pour any remaining vinegar mixture over the beef. Cover and refrigerate for 4-6 hours, or overnight.
4. **Dry the Meat**: Remove the beef from the marinade and pat dry with paper towels. Arrange the strips on a wire rack or hang them in a well-ventilated area. Ensure there is enough space between each strip for air to circulate.
5. **Drying Process**: Allow the beef to air dry for 3-7 days, depending on your preferred dryness and the humidity of your environment. A dedicated biltong box with a fan and light can speed up the process.
6. **Store and Serve**: Once dried to your liking, slice the biltong thinly against the grain. Store in an airtight container. Enjoy as a snack or use in various dishes.

Chapter 10: Mandazi

- East African doughnuts that are lightly sweetened, flavored with coconut milk, and deep-fried until golden and fluffy.

Ingredients:

- 2 cups all-purpose flour
- 1/4 cup sugar
- 2 teaspoons baking powder
- 1/4 teaspoon salt
- 1 teaspoon ground cardamom (optional)
- 1/2 cup coconut milk (or regular milk)
- 1 large egg
- 2 tablespoons melted butter or vegetable oil
- 1/2 teaspoon vanilla extract
- Vegetable oil for frying
- Powdered sugar for dusting (optional)

Cooking Instructions:

1. **Mix Dry Ingredients**: In a large bowl, combine the flour, sugar, baking powder, salt, and ground cardamom (if using). Mix well.
2. **Combine Wet Ingredients**: In a separate bowl, whisk together the coconut milk, egg, melted butter (or vegetable oil), and vanilla extract until well combined.
3. **Form the Dough**: Gradually add the wet ingredients to the dry ingredients, mixing until a dough forms. The dough should be soft but not sticky. If necessary, add a little

more flour or milk to achieve the right consistency.
4. **Rest the Dough**: Cover the dough with a clean cloth and let it rest for 30 minutes.
5. **Roll Out the Dough**: On a lightly floured surface, roll out the dough to about 1/4 inch thickness. Using a knife or a dough cutter, cut the dough into triangles, squares, or circles.
6. **Heat the Oil**: In a deep skillet or frying pan, heat the vegetable oil over medium-high heat until it reaches 350°F (175°C). To test the oil, drop a small piece of dough into the oil; if it sizzles and rises to the surface, the oil is ready.
7. **Fry the Mandazi**: Carefully place a few pieces of dough into the hot oil, being careful not to overcrowd the pan. Fry until golden brown, about 2-3 minutes per side. Use a slotted spoon to remove the mandazi from the oil and drain on paper towels.
8. **Dust with Sugar**: If desired, dust the warm mandazi with powdered sugar.
9. **Serve**: Serve the mandazi warm or at room temperature. They can be enjoyed on their own or with a cup of tea or coffee.

Chapter 11: Kachumbari

- A fresh, tangy salad from East Africa, made with tomatoes, onions, and cilantro, often spiced with chili and lemon juice.

Ingredients:

- 4 ripe tomatoes, finely chopped
- 1 large red onion, finely sliced
- 1 cucumber, peeled and finely chopped
- 1-2 fresh chili peppers, finely chopped (optional)
- 1/4 cup fresh cilantro, chopped
- Juice of 2 limes
- Salt to taste
- 1 avocado, diced (optional)
- 1 teaspoon olive oil (optional)

Cooking Instructions:

1. **Prepare the Vegetables**: In a large bowl, combine the chopped tomatoes, sliced red onion, and chopped cucumber.
2. **Add Chili and Cilantro**: If using, add the finely chopped chili peppers to the bowl. Stir in the chopped fresh cilantro.
3. **Dress the Salad**: Squeeze the lime juice over the salad and season with salt to taste. If desired, add the diced avocado and a teaspoon of olive oil for extra richness.
4. **Toss and Serve**: Gently toss all the ingredients together until well combined. Serve immediately as a fresh and vibrant side dish.

Chapter 12: Chakalaka

- A South African vegetable relish made with onions, tomatoes, carrots, beans, and spices, typically served with bread, pap, or grilled meats.

Ingredients:

- 2 tablespoons vegetable oil
- 1 large onion, chopped
- 2 cloves garlic, minced
- 1 red bell pepper, chopped
- 1 green bell pepper, chopped
- 2 large carrots, grated
- 2 large tomatoes, chopped
- 1 can (15 ounces) baked beans in tomato sauce
- 1 teaspoon curry powder
- 1 teaspoon smoked paprika
- 1/2 teaspoon chili powder (optional)
- Salt and pepper to taste
- 1/4 cup chopped fresh parsley or cilantro

Cooking Instructions:

1. **Cook the Onions**: In a large skillet or pot, heat the vegetable oil over medium heat. Add the chopped onions and sauté until they become translucent.
2. **Add Garlic and Peppers**: Add the minced garlic, chopped red bell pepper, and chopped green bell pepper to the skillet. Cook for about 5 minutes until the peppers start to soften.

3. **Add Carrots and Tomatoes**: Stir in the grated carrots and chopped tomatoes. Cook for another 5-7 minutes, allowing the vegetables to soften and the tomatoes to break down.
4. **Spice It Up**: Add the curry powder, smoked paprika, and chili powder (if using). Stir well to combine the spices with the vegetables.
5. **Add Baked Beans**: Pour in the can of baked beans in tomato sauce. Stir everything together and bring the mixture to a simmer.
6. **Season and Simmer**: Season with salt and pepper to taste. Let the chakalaka simmer for about 10-15 minutes, stirring occasionally, until the flavors meld together.
7. **Finish and Serve**: Stir in the chopped fresh parsley or cilantro just before serving. Serve the chakalaka hot as a side dish with bread, rice, or as a topping for grilled meats.

Chapter 13: Moambe Chicken

- A flavorful Congolese stew made with chicken, palm butter, and a blend of spices, served with rice or fufu.

Ingredients:

- 1 whole chicken, cut into pieces
- 1/4 cup palm oil or vegetable oil
- 2 large onions, finely chopped
- 4 cloves garlic, minced
- 1-inch piece of ginger, grated
- 1 red bell pepper, chopped
- 2 tomatoes, chopped
- 1/2 cup tomato paste
- 1 cup chicken broth
- 1/2 cup moambe (palm nut) sauce or peanut butter
- 2-3 scotch bonnet peppers, whole (optional)
- 1 teaspoon smoked paprika
- Salt and pepper to taste
- 1/2 cup chopped spinach or other leafy greens
- Fresh parsley or cilantro for garnish

Cooking Instructions:

1. **Prepare the Chicken**: Season the chicken pieces with salt and pepper. In a large pot, heat the palm oil or vegetable oil over medium-high heat. Brown the chicken pieces on all sides, working in batches if necessary. Remove the chicken and set aside.

2. **Cook the Aromatics**: In the same pot, add the chopped onions and sauté until golden brown. Add the minced garlic and grated ginger, and cook for another 2-3 minutes until fragrant.
3. **Add Vegetables**: Add the chopped red bell pepper and cook until it starts to soften, about 3-4 minutes.
4. **Tomato Mixture**: Stir in the chopped tomatoes and tomato paste. Cook this mixture, stirring occasionally, until it reduces and the oil starts to separate from the tomato mixture (about 10-15 minutes).
5. **Combine Ingredients**: Return the browned chicken pieces to the pot. Pour in the chicken broth and bring to a boil.
6. **Add Moambe Sauce**: Reduce the heat to low and stir in the moambe sauce or peanut butter until well combined. Add the whole scotch bonnet peppers if using. Add the smoked paprika. Simmer the mixture for about 30 minutes, until the chicken is cooked through and tender.
7. **Finish the Dish**: Stir in the chopped spinach or other leafy greens and cook for an additional 5-10 minutes until the greens are wilted and tender.
8. **Season and Serve**: Adjust seasoning with salt and pepper to taste. Remove the scotch bonnet peppers before serving if a milder dish is desired. Garnish with fresh parsley or cilantro. Serve hot with rice, fufu, or boiled plantains.

Chapter 14: Groundnut Stew

- A creamy West African stew made with peanuts, tomatoes, onions, and a variety of meats or vegetables, served with rice or couscous.

Ingredients:

- 2 tablespoons vegetable oil
- 1 large onion, chopped
- 3 cloves garlic, minced
- 1-inch piece of ginger, grated
- 1 red bell pepper, chopped
- 2 large tomatoes, chopped
- 1/2 cup tomato paste
- 1 cup peanut butter (smooth or chunky)
- 4 cups chicken or vegetable broth
- 1 lb (450g) chicken thighs or beef, cut into bite-sized pieces (optional)
- 2-3 sweet potatoes, peeled and cubed
- 1 teaspoon ground cumin
- 1 teaspoon ground coriander
- 1/2 teaspoon cayenne pepper (optional)
- Salt and pepper to taste
- 2 cups chopped kale or spinach
- 1/4 cup chopped fresh cilantro or parsley for garnish
- Chopped peanuts for garnish (optional)

Cooking Instructions:

1. **Prepare the Meat**: If using meat, season the chicken or beef pieces with salt and pepper. In a large pot, heat the vegetable oil

over medium-high heat. Brown the meat on all sides, then remove and set aside.
2. **Cook the Aromatics**: In the same pot, add the chopped onion and sauté until golden brown. Add the minced garlic and grated ginger, and cook for another 2-3 minutes until fragrant.
3. **Add Vegetables**: Add the chopped red bell pepper and cook until it starts to soften, about 3-4 minutes. Stir in the chopped tomatoes and tomato paste. Cook this mixture, stirring occasionally, until it reduces and the oil starts to separate from the tomato mixture (about 10-15 minutes).
4. **Combine Ingredients**: Return the browned meat to the pot (if using). Pour in the chicken or vegetable broth and bring to a boil. Stir in the peanut butter until well combined. Add the cubed sweet potatoes, ground cumin, ground coriander, and cayenne pepper (if using).
5. **Simmer**: Reduce the heat to low and simmer the stew for about 30 minutes, or until the sweet potatoes are tender and the flavors have melded together. Stir occasionally to prevent sticking.
6. **Add Greens**: Stir in the chopped kale or spinach and cook for an additional 5-10 minutes until the greens are wilted and tender.
7. **Season and Serve**: Adjust seasoning with salt and pepper to taste. Serve the groundnut stew hot, garnished with chopped fresh cilantro or parsley and chopped peanuts if desired. Enjoy with rice, couscous, or flatbread.

Chapter 15: Braaibroodjies

- South African grilled sandwiches made with cheese, tomato, and onion, traditionally cooked over a braai (barbecue).

Ingredients:

- 8 slices of white or whole wheat bread
- 4 tablespoons butter, softened
- 1 cup grated cheddar cheese
- 1 large tomato, thinly sliced
- 1 small red onion, thinly sliced
- 1 tablespoon chutney (optional)
- Salt and pepper to taste

Cooking Instructions:

1. **Prepare the Bread**: Spread a thin layer of butter on one side of each slice of bread.
2. **Assemble the Sandwiches**: On the unbuttered side of four slices of bread, layer the grated cheddar cheese, tomato slices, and red onion slices. If using, spread a thin layer of chutney on the top slice of bread. Season with salt and pepper to taste.
3. **Top with Bread**: Place the remaining slices of bread on top of the filling, buttered side up, to form sandwiches.
4. **Grill the Sandwiches**: Heat a grill or braai to medium heat. Place the sandwiches on the grill, buttered side down. Grill for 3-5 minutes on each side, or until the bread is golden brown and the cheese is melted.

5. **Serve**: Remove the sandwiches from the grill and let them cool slightly. Cut them in half and serve warm.

Chapter 16: Fufu and Light Soup

- A staple in Ghanaian cuisine, fufu is a dough-like side dish made from cassava or plantains, served with a light and spicy tomato-based soup.

Fufu Ingredients:

- 2 cups cassava flour (or yam flour)
- 4 cups water

Fufu Cooking Instructions:

1. **Boil the Water**: In a large pot, bring the water to a boil.
2. **Add Flour**: Gradually add the cassava flour to the boiling water, stirring continuously to prevent lumps.
3. **Cook the Fufu**: Reduce the heat to low and continue to stir the mixture vigorously for 10-15 minutes until it becomes smooth and stretchy. The fufu should have a dough-like consistency.
4. **Shape the Fufu**: Remove the fufu from the heat and shape it into small balls or mounds using a spoon or your hands (wet your hands with water to prevent sticking).
5. **Serve**: Serve the fufu warm with light soup.

Light Soup Ingredients:

- 1 lb (450g) goat meat, chicken, or fish, cut into pieces
- 1 large onion, chopped
- 3 cloves garlic, minced

- 1-inch piece of ginger, grated
- 2 large tomatoes, chopped
- 2 tablespoons tomato paste
- 1 fresh chili pepper, chopped (optional)
- 4 cups water or chicken broth
- 1 tablespoon ground crayfish (optional)
- Salt and pepper to taste
- Fresh cilantro or parsley for garnish

Light Soup Cooking Instructions:

1. **Prepare the Meat**: In a large pot, combine the meat with the chopped onion, minced garlic, and grated ginger. Add enough water to cover the meat and bring to a boil. Reduce the heat and simmer until the meat is tender, about 30-45 minutes. Remove the meat and set aside. Reserve the broth.
2. **Cook the Tomatoes**: In the same pot, add the chopped tomatoes, tomato paste, and chili pepper (if using). Cook for about 10-15 minutes until the tomatoes break down and form a thick sauce.
3. **Combine Ingredients**: Return the cooked meat to the pot. Add the reserved broth and additional water or chicken broth to reach the desired soup consistency. Stir in the ground crayfish (if using).
4. **Simmer the Soup**: Bring the soup to a boil, then reduce the heat and simmer for 20-30 minutes, allowing the flavors to meld together.
5. **Season and Serve**: Season the soup with salt and pepper to taste. Garnish with fresh cilantro or parsley. Serve hot with fufu.

Chapter 17: Sosaties

- South African kebabs made with marinated meat (often lamb) and dried apricots, skewered and grilled to perfection.

Ingredients:

- 8 slices of white or whole wheat bread
- 4 tablespoons butter, softened
- 1 cup grated cheddar cheese
- 1 large tomato, thinly sliced
- 1 small red onion, thinly sliced
- 1 tablespoon chutney (optional)
- Salt and pepper to taste

Cooking Instructions:

1. **Prepare the Bread**: Spread a thin layer of butter on one side of each slice of bread.
2. **Assemble the Sandwiches**: On the unbuttered side of four slices of bread, layer the grated cheddar cheese, tomato slices, and red onion slices. If using, spread a thin layer of chutney on the top slice of bread. Season with salt and pepper to taste.
3. **Top with Bread**: Place the remaining slices of bread on top of the filling, buttered side up, to form sandwiches.
4. **Grill the Sandwiches**: Heat a grill or braai to medium heat. Place the sandwiches on the grill, buttered side down. Grill for 3-5 minutes on each side, or until the bread is golden brown and the cheese is melted.

5. **Serve**: Remove the sandwiches from the grill and let them cool slightly. Cut them in half and serve warm.

Chapter 18: Sambaza

- A popular Rwandan dish made with fried small fish (similar to sardines), typically served with a side of plantains or rice.

Ingredients:

- 1 lb (450g) fresh sardines (Sambaza), cleaned and scaled
- 1 cup all-purpose flour
- 1 teaspoon paprika
- 1 teaspoon garlic powder
- 1 teaspoon onion powder
- 1/2 teaspoon ground black pepper
- 1/2 teaspoon salt
- Vegetable oil for frying
- Lemon wedges for serving
- Fresh parsley or cilantro for garnish

Cooking Instructions:

1. **Prepare the Coating**: In a shallow dish, combine the all-purpose flour, paprika, garlic powder, onion powder, ground black pepper, and salt. Mix well.
2. **Coat the Sardines**: Pat the cleaned sardines dry with paper towels. Dredge each sardine in the seasoned flour mixture, shaking off any excess flour.
3. **Heat the Oil**: In a large frying pan, heat about 1/2 inch of vegetable oil over medium-high heat until hot but not smoking. To test if the oil is ready, drop a small piece

of bread into the oil; if it sizzles and browns, the oil is ready.
4. **Fry the Sardines**: Carefully place the coated sardines into the hot oil in a single layer. Fry for about 3-4 minutes on each side, or until golden brown and crispy. Do not overcrowd the pan; fry in batches if necessary.
5. **Drain the Sardines**: Use a slotted spoon to remove the fried sardines from the oil and place them on a paper towel-lined plate to drain any excess oil.
6. **Serve**: Arrange the fried sardines on a serving platter. Garnish with fresh parsley or cilantro and serve with lemon wedges. Enjoy hot as a snack or appetizer.

Chapter 19: Waakye

- A Ghanaian dish of rice and beans cooked together with millet leaves, served with a variety of accompaniments like fried plantains, spaghetti, and boiled eggs.

Ingredients:

- 2 cups rice (preferably jasmine or basmati)
- 1 cup black-eyed peas or red beans
- 2-3 dried millet leaves (optional, for authentic color)
- 1 teaspoon baking soda (optional, for authentic color)
- 6 cups water
- 1 large onion, chopped
- 2 cloves garlic, minced
- 1 teaspoon ground ginger
- 1 teaspoon ground cayenne pepper (optional, for heat)
- Salt to taste
- 1/4 cup vegetable oil

Cooking Instructions:

1. **Prepare the Beans**: Rinse the black-eyed peas or red beans and place them in a large pot with 4 cups of water. Add the dried millet leaves and baking soda if using. Bring to a boil, then reduce the heat and simmer for about 45 minutes to 1 hour, or until the beans are tender. Remove the millet leaves and drain the beans.

2. **Cook the Aromatics**: In the same pot, heat the vegetable oil over medium heat. Add the chopped onion and sauté until translucent. Add the minced garlic and cook for another 1-2 minutes until fragrant.
3. **Combine Ingredients**: Add the drained beans back to the pot along with the rice. Stir in the ground ginger, cayenne pepper (if using), and salt to taste.
4. **Cook the Rice and Beans**: Add 6 cups of water to the pot and bring to a boil. Reduce the heat to low, cover the pot, and simmer for about 20-25 minutes, or until the rice is cooked and the water is absorbed. Stir occasionally to prevent sticking.
5. **Serve**: Remove the pot from the heat and let it sit, covered, for 5-10 minutes. Fluff the Waakye with a fork and serve hot, traditionally accompanied by fried plantains, boiled eggs, and shito (Ghanaian hot pepper sauce).

Chapter 20: Couscous

- A North African staple, couscous is steamed semolina granules served with a hearty stew of meat and vegetables, often flavored with saffron and other spices.

Ingredients:

- 2 cups couscous
- 2 cups water or chicken broth
- 2 tablespoons olive oil
- 1 teaspoon salt
- 1/2 teaspoon ground black pepper
- 1/2 teaspoon ground cumin
- 1/4 teaspoon ground cinnamon
- 1/4 cup raisins (optional)
- 1/4 cup chopped almonds or pine nuts (optional)
- 1/4 cup chopped fresh parsley or cilantro
- Juice of 1 lemon

Cooking Instructions:

1. **Boil the Liquid**: In a medium saucepan, bring the water or chicken broth to a boil. Add the salt, ground black pepper, ground cumin, and ground cinnamon. Stir to combine.
2. **Add the Couscous**: Remove the saucepan from the heat and stir in the couscous. Cover the saucepan and let it sit for 5-10 minutes, or until the liquid is absorbed.
3. **Fluff the Couscous**: Use a fork to fluff the couscous, breaking up any clumps.

4. **Add Mix-Ins**: Stir in the olive oil, raisins (if using), chopped almonds or pine nuts (if using), chopped fresh parsley or cilantro, and lemon juice. Mix well to combine.
5. **Serve**: Transfer the couscous to a serving dish and serve warm as a side dish or as a base for stews and tagines. Enjoy!

Conclusion

Thank you for joining us on this culinary adventure through Africa. "20 Classic African Dishes" is more than just a cookbook; it's a gateway to understanding and appreciating the rich tapestry of African culture through its food. By exploring these traditional recipes, you've not only created delicious meals but also connected with the heritage and stories of the people who have cherished these dishes for centuries.

We hope these recipes have inspired you to continue exploring the diverse world of African cuisine. Whether it's the spicy kick of Piri Piri Chicken, the comforting warmth of Egusi Soup, or the aromatic allure of Moroccan Couscous, each dish brings a piece of Africa into your home.

As you continue to experiment and enjoy these dishes, remember that cooking is an act of love and sharing. We encourage you to share these recipes with your family and friends, spreading the joy and flavors of African cuisine. Thank you for being a part of this journey, and may your kitchen always be filled with the vibrant tastes and aromas of Africa.

Made in the USA
Las Vegas, NV
27 August 2024